KOA'E KEA

This book is printed on recycled paper.

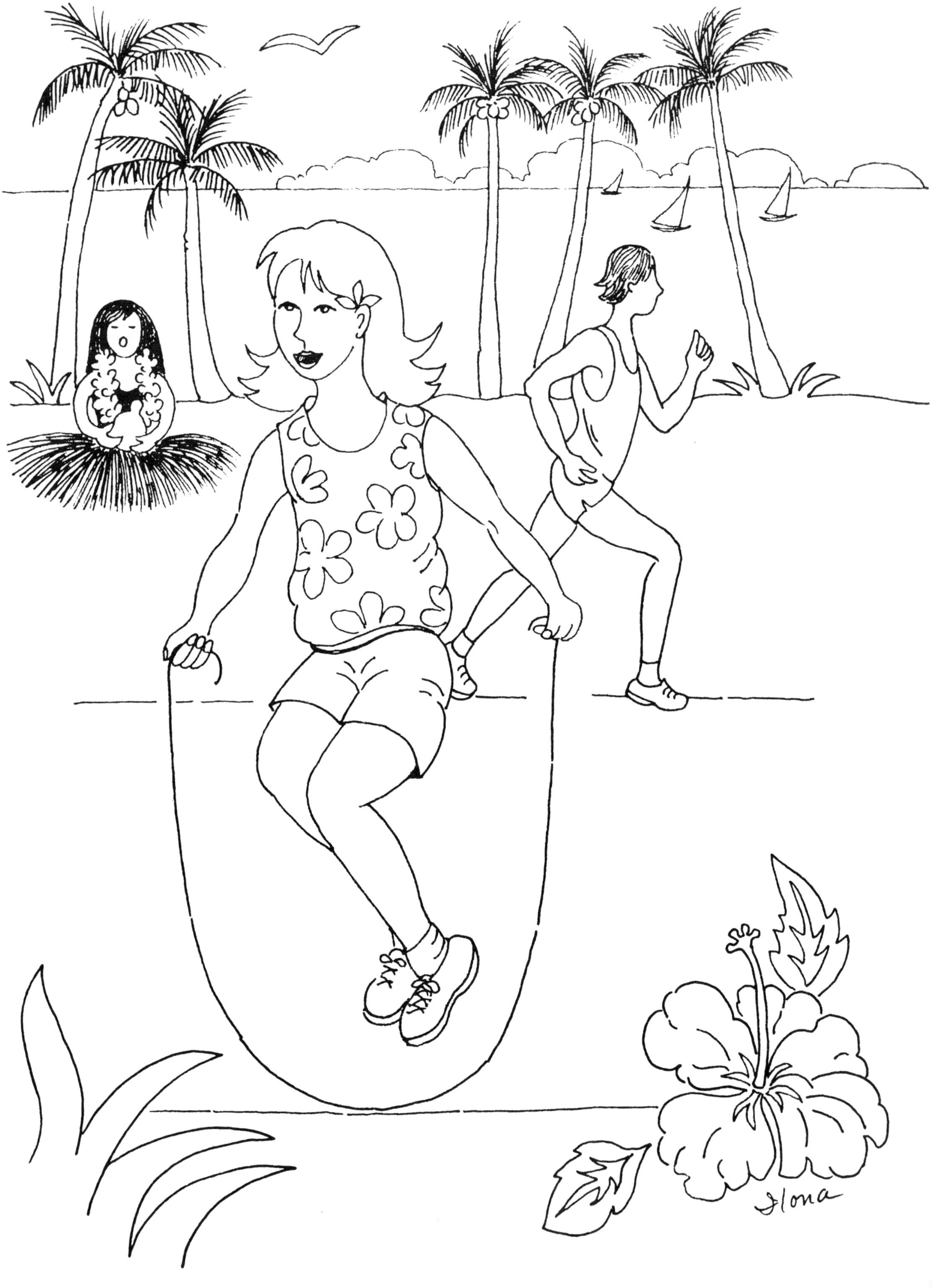
Ilona

From the Album *KOA'E KEA*

SING, GIGGLE, RUN!

Lyrics and Music by Lyn Nanni

In our island home, under sunny skies, children have lots of reasons to SING, GIGGLE AND RUN! But wherever you live, you can always have a song in your heart, a funny bone that giggles and happy feet to run. So sing along with our *KAMALI'I* (children's) chorus and just have fun.

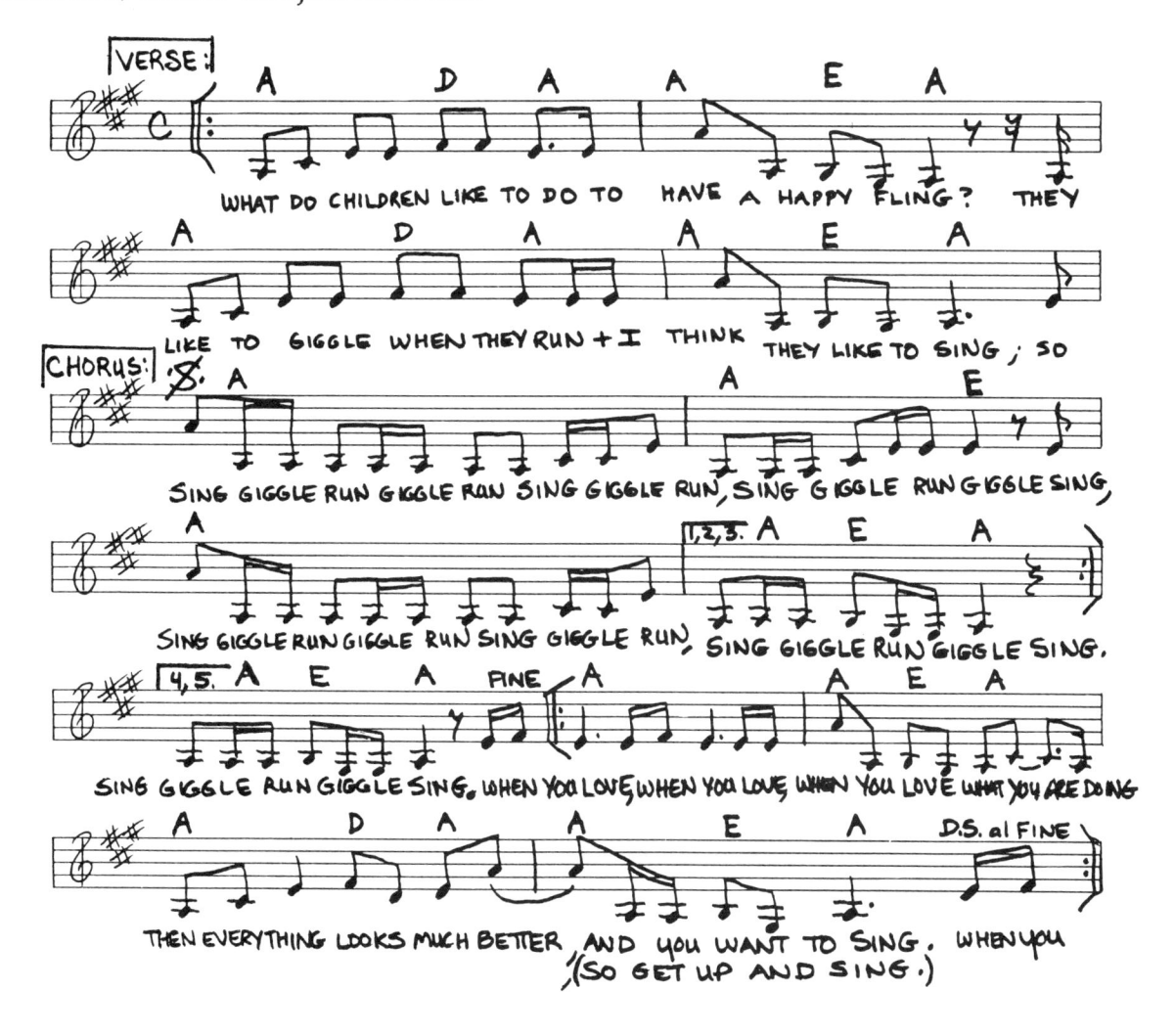

VERSE: What do children like to do to have a happy fling? They like to giggle when they run + I think they like to sing; so

CHORUS: Sing giggle run giggle run sing giggle run, sing giggle run giggle sing, sing giggle run giggle run sing giggle run, sing giggle run giggle sing. Sing giggle run giggle sing, when you love, when you love, when you love what you are doing then everything looks much better, and you want to sing. When you
(So get up and sing.)

VERSE 2: When the day is looking dull, and Mom is doing things, that's the time of day to play the game of giggle, run, sing!

VERSE 3: Birds can fly and fish can jump, and worms are known to wiggle. But children do these three things best, they run and sing and giggle!

VERSE 4: When you love, when you love, when you love what you are doing, then everything looks much better and you want to sing.

VERSE 5: When you love, when you love, when you love what you are doing, then everything looks much better, so get up and sing!

©1991 Lyn Nanni dba Sunset Beach Music, P.O. Box 159, Hale'iwa, Hawai'i 96712

From the Album *KOA'E KEA*

AS SIMPLE AS YOUR A-B-Cs

Lyrics and Music by Lyn Nanni

There is much to learn about people, the world, and where we belong in it. But one thing you don't need to learn from books is that we are all very important to the world; we are all SHINING STARS. It's as SIMPLE AS YOUR A-B-Cs— YOU ARE VERY SPECIAL.

[sheet music: SWING; VERSE: "When you think that someone's better than you, you're feelin' kind of green. It's confused you are, you're a shining star, it's as simple as your ABC's." FINE. CHORUS: "It's time to contemplate ooooooh, how you're doin' great ooooooh, and maybe wait, oooooh, 'till the day gets better, pull yourself together" D.S. al FINE]

VERSE 2: When you think that someone's luck is good, and your's has split the scene, have some faith in you -- do the best you can do -- it's as simple as your ABC's.

VERSE 3: Everytime you go outside, give thanks for all you see. Put a smile on, even tie it on -- it's as simple as your ABC's.

(Last time) I said, as simple as your ABC's -- you bet it is, as simple as your ABC's.....your ABC's!

©1991 Lyn Nanni dba Sunset Beach Music, P.O. Box 159, Hale'iwa, Hawai'i 96712

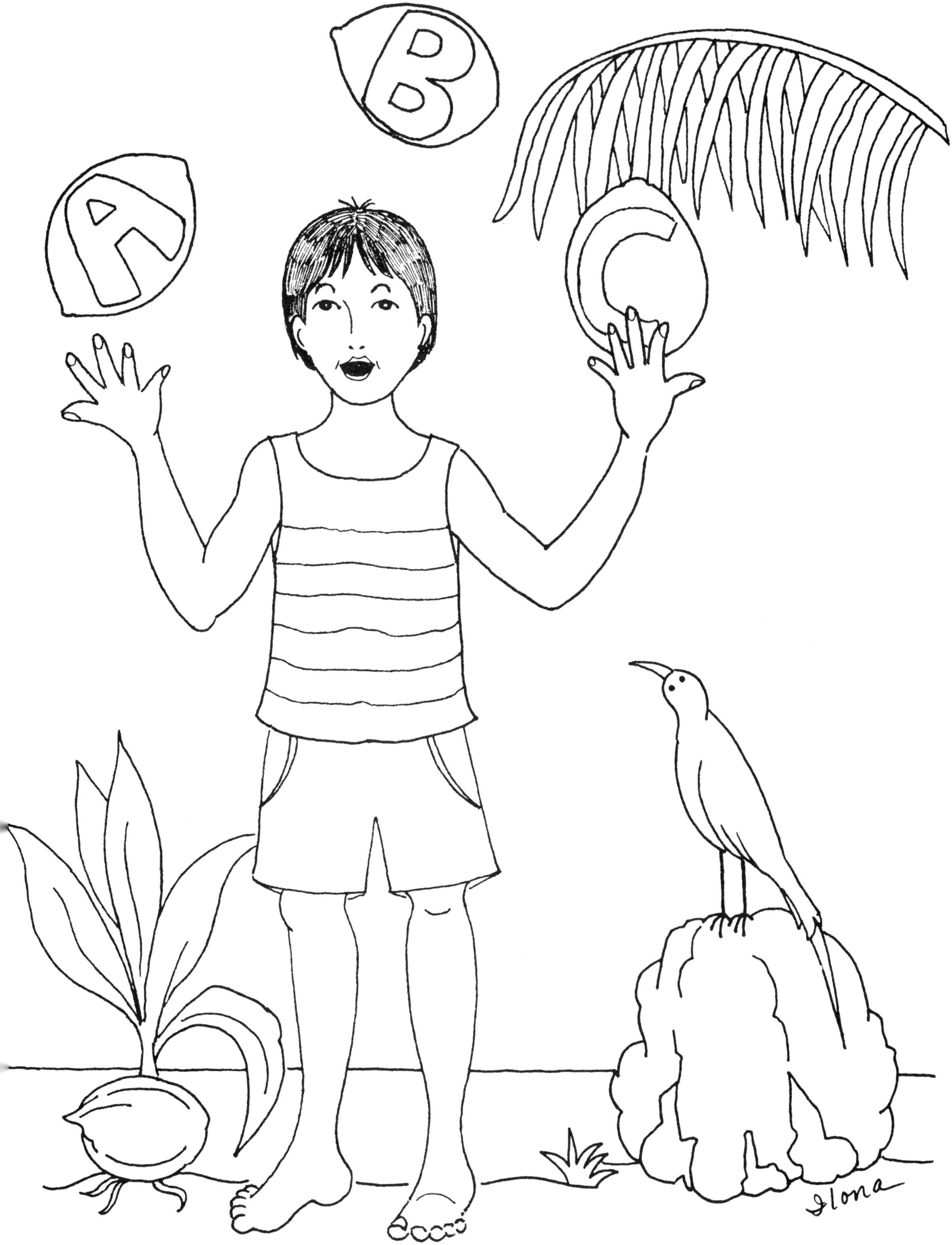
A
B
C
Ilona

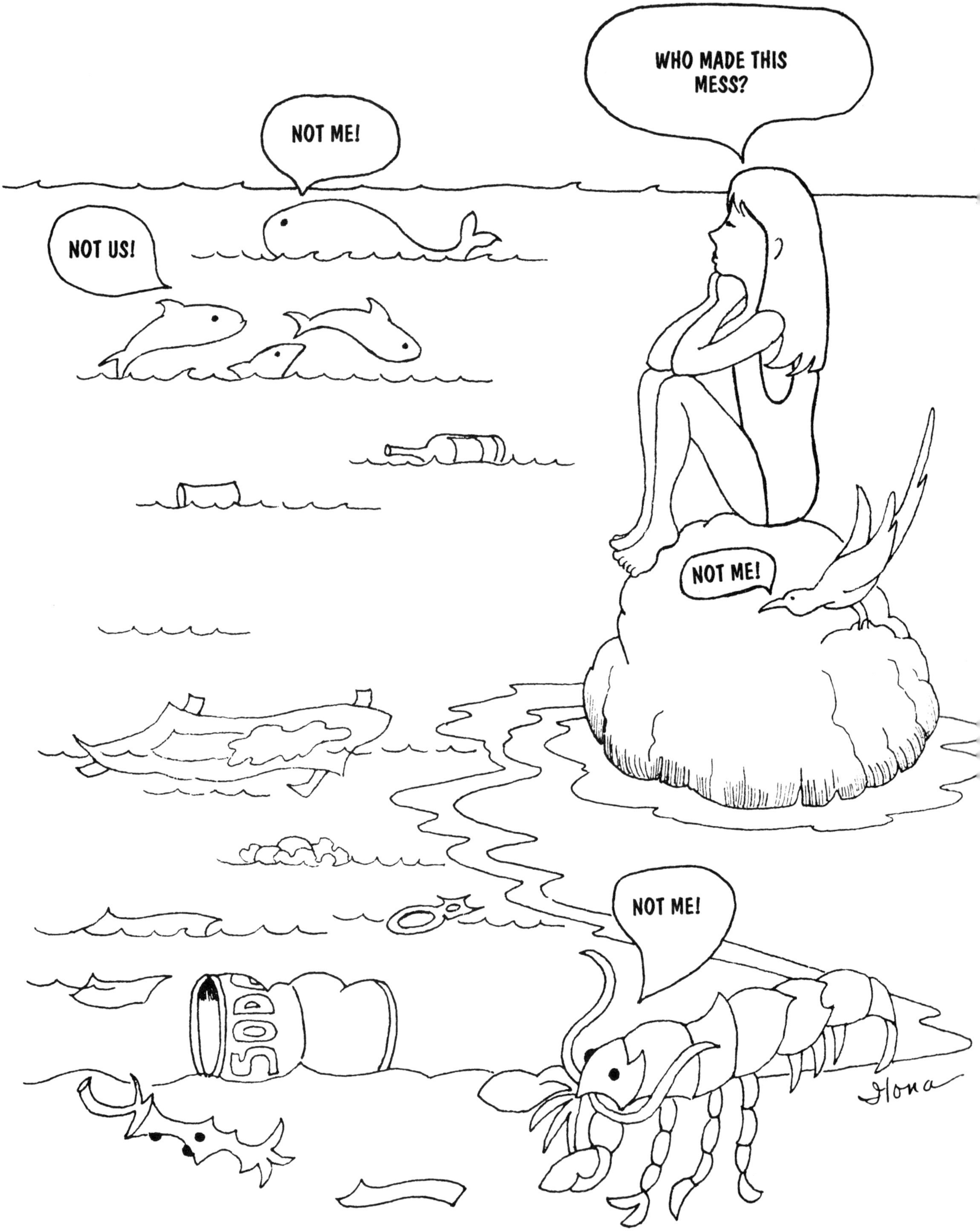
WHO MADE THIS MESS?
NOT ME!
NOT US!
NOT ME!
NOT ME!
SODA
Ilona

From the Album *KOA'E KEA*

WHO MADE THIS MESS?

Lyrics and Music by Lyn Nanni

I know all of you have been told by your moms and dads to CLEAN UP YOUR MESS! Well, we can try NOT to make a mess, but if we do, then WE should clean it up. If someone makes a BIG MESS outside, then that someone should clean up that mess, too, just like you clean your room. The earth is like a giant house where all people and animals have to live, and we <u>all</u> need to keep our rooms clean. Only our "rooms" are the beaches, the rainforests and the skies. So if you see a "messy room" in the earth house, you should ask — "WHO MADE THIS MESS"?

[Musical notation with lyrics:]

BA DA BA BA DA BA BA DA BA BA BA DA BA BA DA BA BA DA BA BA

WHO MADE THIS MESS? I WONDER, WHO MADE THIS MESS? THE FISH IN THE OCEAN WOULD BE SO HAPPY IF WE KEPT OUR GARBAGE OUT OF THE SEA, THE STARS IN THE SKY COULD TWINKLE BRIGHTLY IF POLLUTION WASN'T SO UNSIGHTLY..... WHO MADE THIS MESS? I WONDER, WHO MADE THIS MESS? WHATEVER YOU DO, DON'T YOU MAKE A MESS. BA BA DA BA BA DA BA BA BA DA BA BA DA BA BA DA BA BA DA (VOCAL IMPROVISATION)

VERSE 2: Who made this mess? We need to clean up this mess! We should remember to be thinking that our planet family keeps on shrinking, and all our beaches could be stinking, and smoke in the sky will keep our eye's a-blinking!

VERSE 3: Who made this mess? We need to look at this mess! The trees in the forest need to stay there, so future generations can live and play there. And Mother Earth needs everyone's care, from Honolulu to your own town square!

From the Album *KOA'E KEA*

I WANT TO HELP!

Lyrics and Music by Lyn Nanni

The best thing we can do when we see a mess is to offer to help! Many helping hands are always better and faster than just two. When you help your mom do the yardwork, your yard looks better. When you help clean a beach, you can make many people happy, and save the lives of fishes, dolphins and whales. But the best thing about helping is that it makes us feel good. So always be ready to say — I WANT TO HELP!

CHORUS: I want to help! I want to help! I want to help! I want to help...

VERSE: Someone needs a helping hand today. Someone always has a need. We can be ready at work or play, and this can be our daily creed, yes to help our friends and our family too, the earth around us 'cause we can do it! Anything is possible to all of us and you will get some helping, too! I want to

VERSE 2: There is always something to fix or do, and someone always has the tools. We can look around at our world today and see which of our skills to use! We can mop a floor, we can dig a weed, clean a beach, we can plant a seedling. Each of us can always do a little part, and we can make a difference, too!

©1991 Lyn Nanni dba Sunset Beach Music, P.O. Box 159, Hale'iwa, Hawai'i 96712

'ŌPALA
KEEP HAWAII BEAUTIFUL

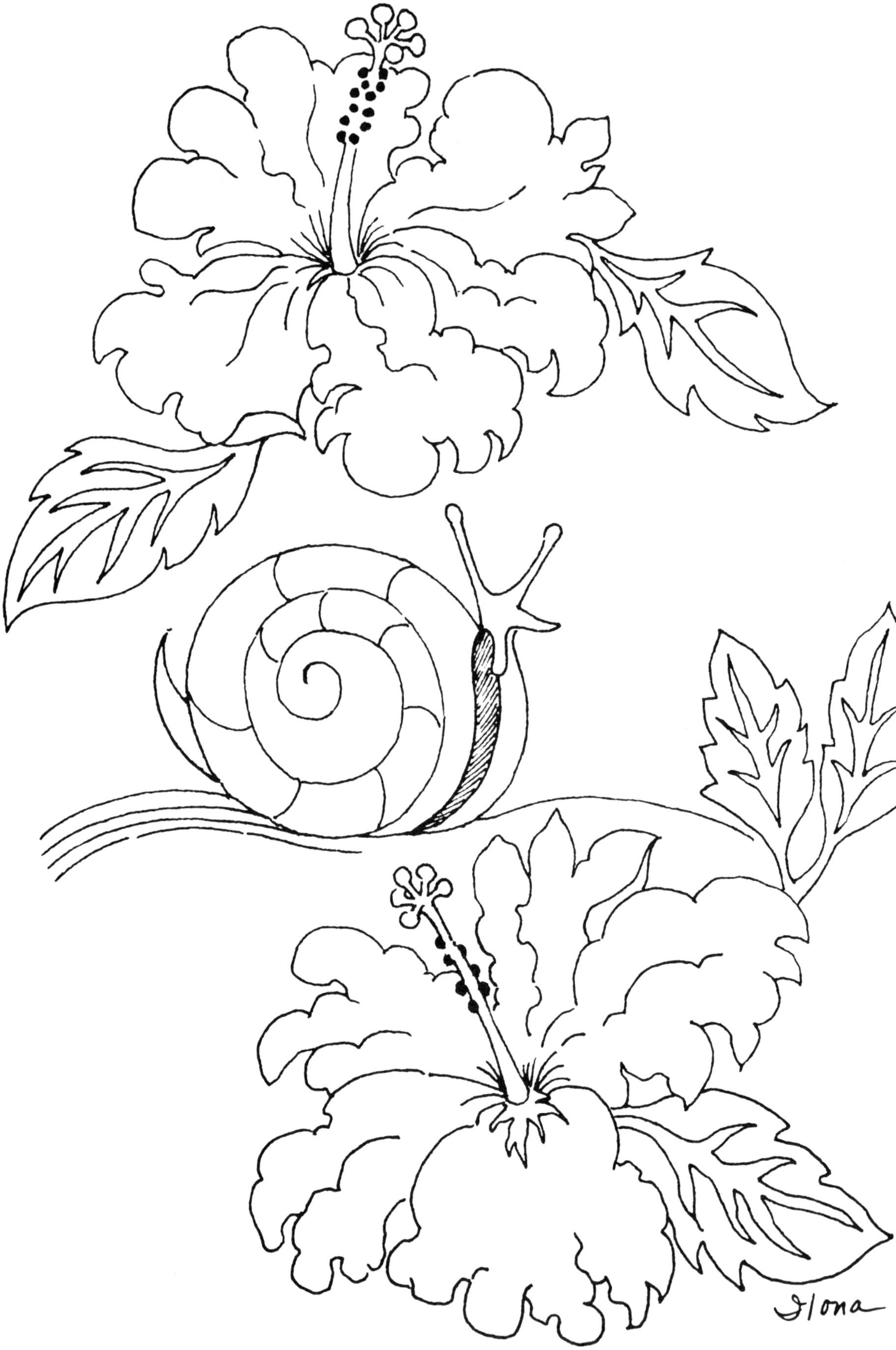
Ilona

From the Album *KOA'E KEA*

THE SNAIL SONG

Lyrics and Music by Lyn Nanni

One name for snail in Hawaiian is *hīhī-wai*. And Hawaiian snails may even be slower than some others because we like to take things easy in the islands. It's hard to tell where our little snail in this song is going, because it takes him so long to get there, but we bid him *ALOHA* (good-bye) and hope to see him again on the lawn someday.

[Sheet music with lyrics:]

VERSE: I saw that snail crawling up the wall, he was going very slow. So I said to myself, how fast do you think that little snail could go? The answer would have to be, my-self I said to me. The fastest a snail could go is very slow.

CHORUS: Snails come, snails go, snails crawl very slow. Snails come, snails go, snails crawl very.... slow, very.... slow......

VERSE 2: All by himself he was crawling, so I wondered where he'd go? Did he have a mom and a dad and a sister that would miss him so? That snail he looked at me -- he smiled and showed his teeth! He seemed to understand what I did not know.

VERSE 3: Now down the shelf he was crawling so I watched him carry on. Antennaes up in the air, his little shell still fastened on. For me it was time to go...but I would like to know, can we meet again someday upon the lawn?

©1991 Lyn Nanni dba Sunset Beach Music, P.O. Box 159, Hale'iwa, Hawai'i 96712

From the Album *KOA'E KEA*

KOA'E KEA (White-tailed tropic bird)

Lyrics and Music by Lyn Nanni

Along the windward cliffs and inland valleys of our islands flies a beautiful white-tailed tropic bird called ***Koa'e kea***. Her flight is graceful and her tail flows out behind as she soars upward on the currents of the wind. *Koa'e kea* can see for many miles from her place in the sky, and looking down at the sea, winking like a beautiful emerald jewel, she can see the many fish, turtles, dolphins and whales, all of her friends of the ocean. She might sing a song for you that goes like this:

[Sheet music with chorus and verse]

CHORUS: I AM FREE I SAIL THE SKIES ALL DAY. I'M A FLYING SAILOR, I AM KEA, KOA'E KEA....

VERSE: CRYSTAL BLUE OCEAN WINKS DOWN BELOW. HEAVENS ABOVE, IT'S SO GREAT TO BE SO FREE......... I AM FREE, I AM KEA, KOA'E KEA......

CHORUS: I am free, I ride the currents to play -- I'm a breath of wind, I am Kea, Koa'e Kea.

VERSE 2: I see my friends lying in the sun -- while I glide high above, having fun.....fun. I am free, I am Kea, Koa'e Kea.

VERSE 3: High mountain cliffs, they are calling me. Valleys below them all lead to the sea.....the sea.

CHORUS: I am free, I sail the skies all day. I'm a flying sailor, I am Kea, Koa'e Kea.

©1991 Lyn Nanni dba Sunset Beach Music, P.O. Box 159, Hale'iwa, Hawai'i 96712

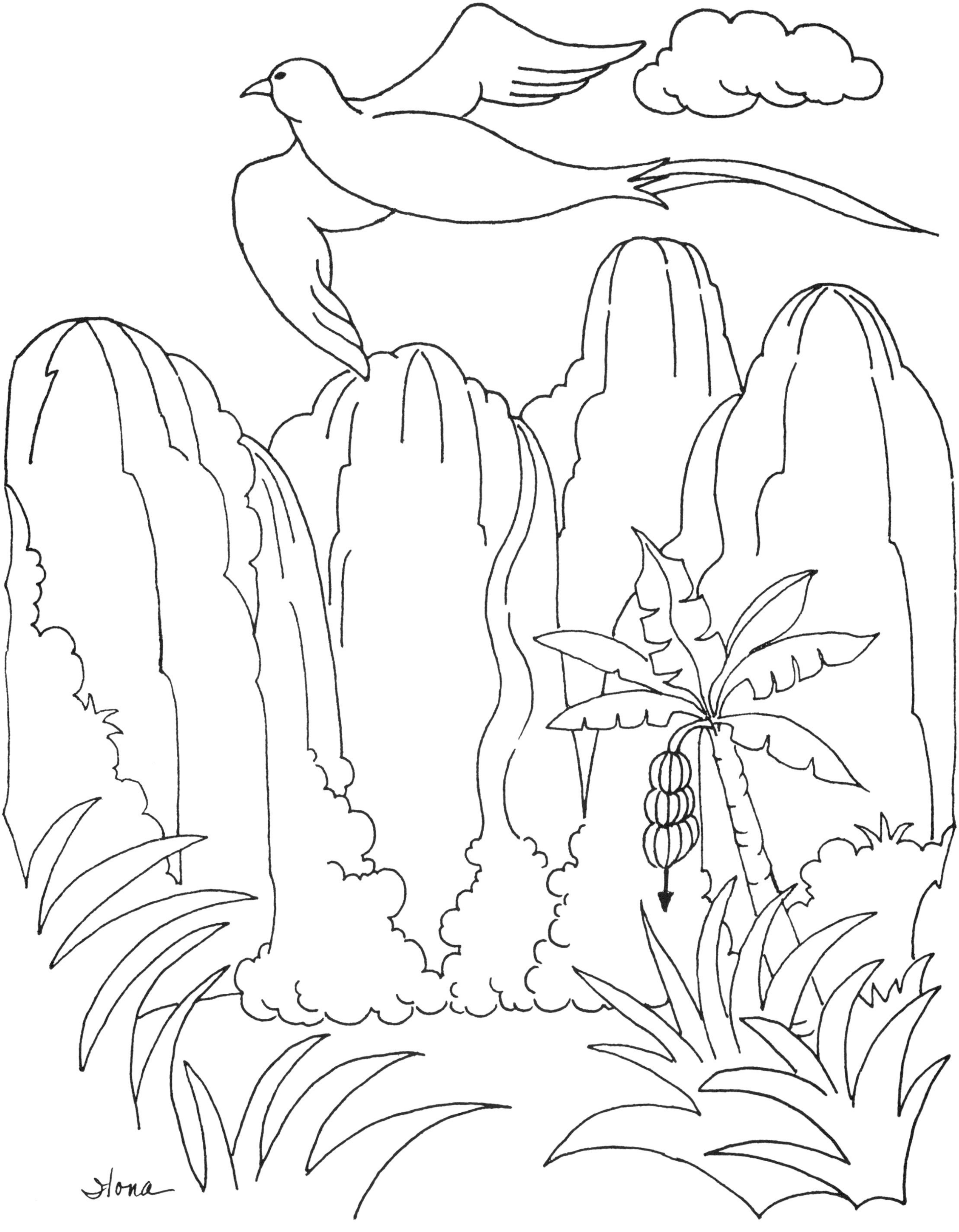
Ilona

Hawaiian Cleaner Wrasse

From the Album *KOA'E KEA*

ONE LITTLE FISH

Lyrics and Music by Lyn Nanni

This song is about a small fish found around Hawaiian reefs known as the "cleaner wrasse." They are brilliantly colored with yellow, black and violet stripes and they serve a very special purpose. They "clean" tiny parasites from other fish by <u>eating</u> the parasites. The fishes who suffer from these parasites will even "form a line" to wait for the cleaner wrasse to rid them of their "itch." So you see, "one little fish" can be <u>very</u> important to many other fishes in the ocean.

[VERSE:] I AM ONE LITTLE FISH + IT SEEMS I AM NOTHING, JUST ONE LITTLE FISH + I FEEL SO VERY SMALL, YES I AM ONE LITTLE FISH BUT I CAN TRY TO BE BIGGER, I CAN SWISH MY FINS PROUDLY 'TILL IT SEEMS I AM TALL. [CHORUS] EVERYDAY I FEEL MYSELF GROWING. IF I ONLY CAN BELIEVE, ALL MY DREAMS WILL COME TO ME.

(ONE) VERY LITTLE FISH BUT A BIG PART OF MY WORLD ....

VERSE 2: I am one little fish, but my life is important. I'm a very special part of the chain of life for all. Yes, I am one little fish, and I always will be something, one very little fish, but my part is not so small.

VERSE 3: I am one little fish, surrounded by an ocean, a huge sea of wonders that waves and rolls and swirls. Yes, I am one little fish but I always will be something, one very little fish but a big part of the world. One very little fish but a big part of the world!

©1991 Lyn Nanni dba Sunset Beach Music, P.O. Box 159, Hale'iwa, Hawai'i 96712

From the Album *KOA'E KEA*

LITTLE GENTLE ROLLING WAVE

Lyrics and Music by Lyn Nanni

In Hawai'i, we see wonders around us every day — rainbows and mountain cliffs covered by deep green carpets of life. But of all the beauty in the islands, the sea is most important in so many ways. It gives us food and cool breezes over the water and the gifts of canoeing, swimming, surfing and sailing. We <u>all</u> must protect this ocean and treat it with love and care at all times. When you are watching the waves on the ocean and enjoying its beauty, you can think of this song......

VERSE:

Little gentle rolling wave out upon the ocean, rolling in a line at sea.

Little gentle rolling wave, moving all the time, reminds me of the love, the love that's yours + mine, the love that we can feel + see. (when I

CHORUS:

sit at the edge of the wave, then I think of the beauty that's here and I hope that this wonder can be saved, for all time, for all time...

Little gentle rolling wave (O ka nalu iki)

Little gentle rolling wave (O ka nalu iki) little gentle rolling wave-ooo.

©1991 Lyn Nanni dba Sunset Beach Music, P.O. Box 159, Hale'iwa, Hawai'i 96712

VERSE 2: Little gentle rolling wave out upon the ocean, rolling in a line at sea. Little gentle rolling wave, softer than a sigh. My face begins to smile, it's like a lullaby, a lullaby that's sung for me.

VERSE 3: 'Oni ana mālie, 'o ka nalu iki, 'oni lālani i ke kai. 'Oni ana mālie, 'o ka nalu iki, nānaina alai maka, ka nalu kai 'ale'a, hāwanawana mai ia'u.

Hawaiian lyrics by R. Keoho Fujimoto

Hawaiian translation:
The little wave is moving gently, moving in a line at sea. The little wave is moving gently, a fascinating scene, the soft-voiced wave, whispering to me.

©1991 Lyn Nanni dba Sunset Beach Music, P.O. Box 159, Hale'iwa, Hawai'i 96712

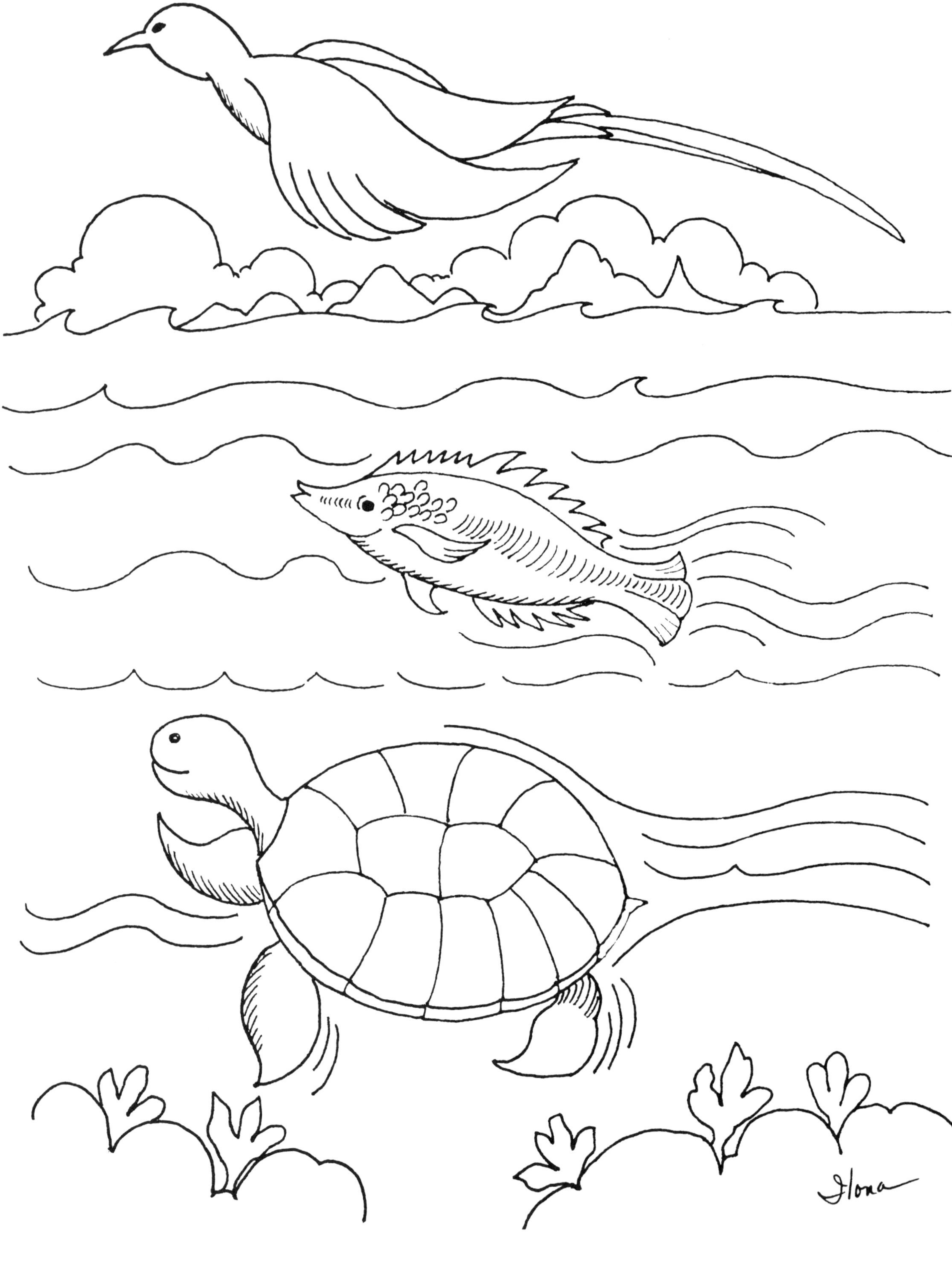
Ilona

From the Album *KOA'E KEA*

WE ARE FRIENDS

Lyrics and Music by Lyn Nanni

This song is about three friends of the ocean and sky: a bird, a turtle and a fish. The bird is KOA'E KEA (white-tailed tropic bird), the turtle is HONU (Hawaiian for sea turtle) and their friend FREDDIE the fish swims on the waves. Imagine these animal friends to be just like you and your friends. Even though they may sing a different song, the language of friends is all the same — it's the LANGUAGE OF LOVE.

[Sheet music with lyrics:]

It's so nice to see you, to see you my friend. You're so helpful to others, you're goodness in expression. You're a bundle of joy + the whole world is a better place, the whole world is so much better 'cause of you. Playing in the ocean keeps us free + so alive. Every wave that lifts us we can feel inside. Kea flies above us, she is calling to the skies, it's a magical world, it's a wonderful life. Call out to each other in the language of love...

VERSE 2: We're three here together, the one who flies the heavens, the green one we call Honu, the one who swims on the waves. We are friends of the ocean and the land and sky above. We are friends, we are love.

VERSE 3: It's so nice to see you, to see you, my friend. We'll swim into the tidepools and back to sea again. While the waves twinkle below us and Kea flies above.....and we call out to each other in the language of love.

©1991 Lyn Nanni dba Sunset Beach Music, P.O. Box 159, Hale'iwa, Hawai'i 96712

From the Album *KOA'E KEA*

LOVE IS KIND

Lyrics and Music by Lyn Nanni

We can always help each other by showing love and kindness. The best place to start this is with your *'OHANA* (family); your brothers, sisters and parents. And when we are patient, kind and loving, we receive the same in return. So if you see someone having a bad day, smile at them and show them that you know — LOVE IS KIND.

[Sheet music with lyrics:]

VERSE: Love is patient + kind. Every-one deserves our love. We take the time to make another feel fine, then we know love is kind.

CHORUS: Sometimes there will be ones who will block your way. Sometimes you must try so very hard. You will find that anything that is worthwhile is worth the price you have to pay........ Love is kind..............

VERSE 2: Love is patient and kind. It's not hard to be this way. We share a smile, help someone on their way, then we brighten their day.

VERSE 3: Love is patient and kind. Everyone deserves our love. We take the time to make another feel fine, then we know love is kind.....love is kind.

©1991 Lyn Nanni dba Sunset Beach Music, P.O. Box 159, Hale'iwa, Hawai'i 96712

Ilona

From the Album *KOA'E KEA*

VISIT THE SEA

Lyrics and Music by Lyn Nanni

Sometimes we don't really appreciate something until we experience it. In this song, this little dolphin can appreciate the ocean because she lives in it. And even though she sometimes thinks that being someone else would be nice, she knows in her heart that the sea is where she belongs. She goes to a different kind of school than you do and she invites you to visit her world and treat it with respect — so, VISIT THE SEA.

[VERSE:]
Visit the sea, visit the world below the ocean. There you'll find me, swirling my fins + worry free, I love my school, I treat my sea world with devotion. I live to swim, I love the colors of the deep.

[CHORUS:]
Sometimes I wish I had feet to run like a child on the street, sometimes I wish that these fins were 2 hands to write letters + play in the sand. But I am me, my world is full of many wonders.... So visit the sea and maybe one day it's you I'll meet. Ooo-ooo-ooo visit the sea visit the sea visit the sea.........

23

From the Album *KOA'E KEA*

LULLABY FOR DUKE

Lyrics and Music by Lyn Nanni

This song is about a very special little boy who loves to fish and collect bugs. Maybe he will grow up to be a scientist and help protect our environment. But for now he likes to play, go to school and hear his mommy sing him a lullaby before he closes his eyes at night. This is a LULLABY FOR DUKE.....

[musical notation with lyrics:]

Mhmm, little boy, the years go by quickly, all of a sudden, you will be a man. I have seen you trying to learn what's around you, with love to surround you I know you'll learn it well. The day you were born your daddy and I, we sang with the night birds 'till the morning light............ Touching for a time............ Hold this to your heart my son, little boy.........

VERSE 2: You like it noisy, I want some quiet. I never know what goes on in your head, but even if I can't understand you, we go hand in hand to face what's up ahead.

VERSE 3: Mmmmm, little boy, our time is so precious. From moment to moment we see each other change. From the son to the father, from daughter to mother, we pass by each other, touching for a time. Hold this to your heart, my son, little boy.

©1991 Lyn Nanni dba Sunset Beach Music, P.O. Box 159, Hale'iwa, Hawai'i 96712

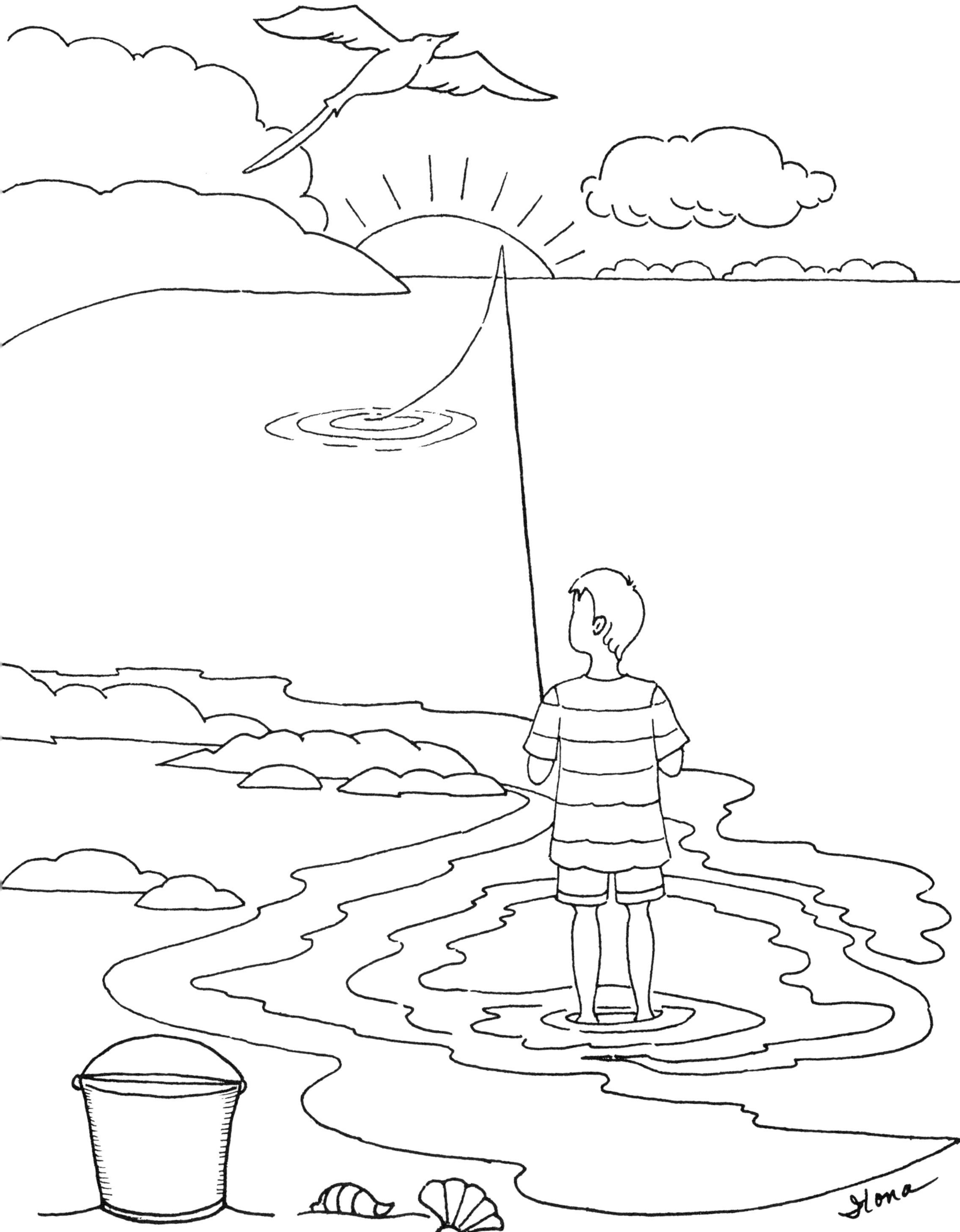
Ilona

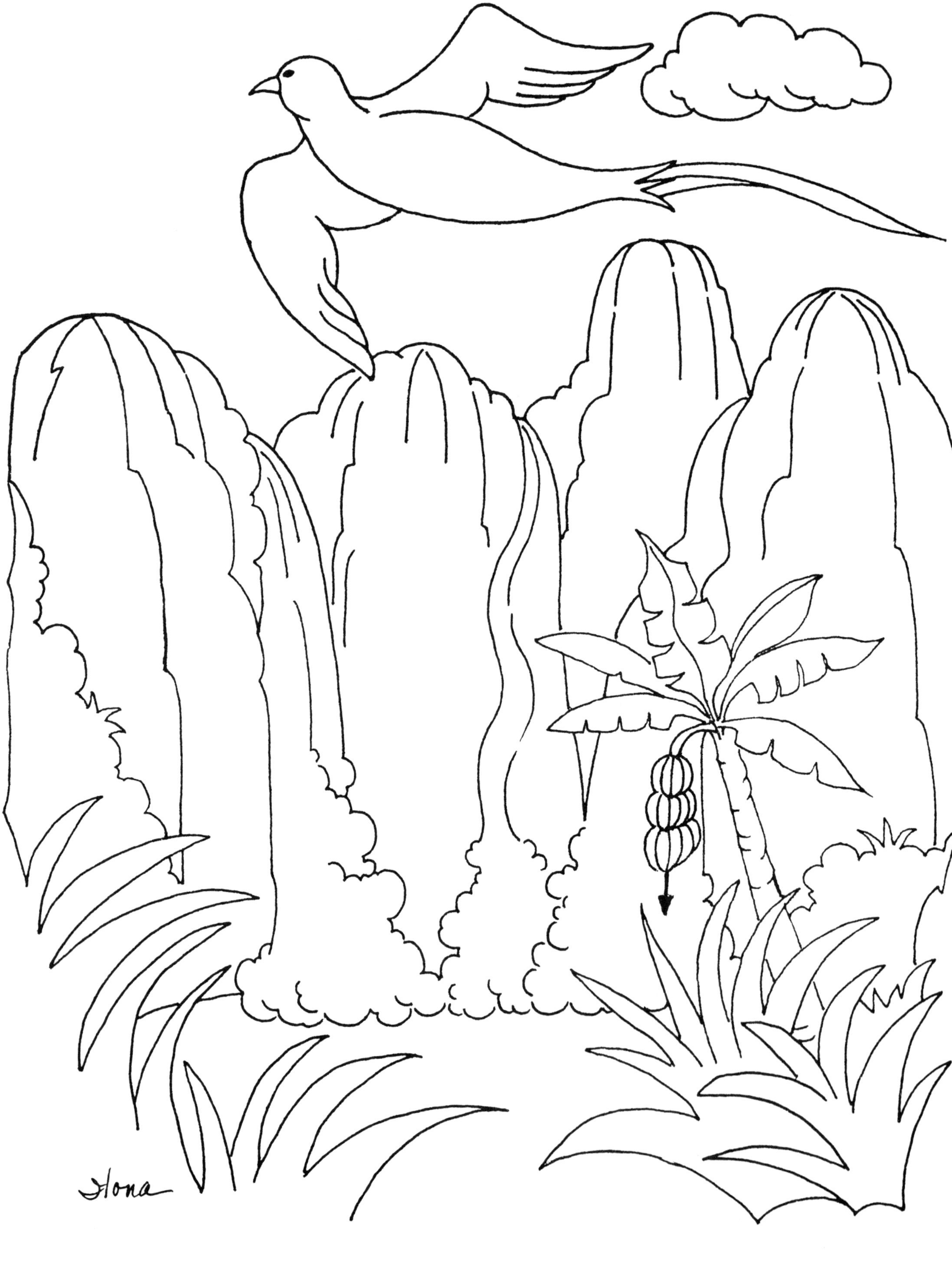
Ilona

Draw a picture of a "Mess" you have seen in your neighborhood...

Draw a picture of how this "Mess" could be cleaned up. . .